QUICK & EASY
FISH AND SEAFOOD

JIM MCCRACKEN

JG
PRESS

Published by
World Publications, Inc.
455 Somerset Avenue
North Dighton, MA 02764

Produced by The Triangle Group, Ltd.
227 Park Avenue
Hoboken, NJ 07030

Editorial: Jake Elwell
Design: Tony Meisel
Printing: Cronion S.A., Barcelona

ISBN 1-57215-004-1

Printed in Spain

Contents

<blockquote>

3
</blockquote>

4

Introduction

Fish and seafood are more popular than ever. Even with the increasing demand and ever-present danger of depleting our marine resources, people are eating more and more different kinds of sea, river and lake creatures. Gone are the days when filets of sole or lobster were the only fishy items at a formal dinner. Now we are eating everything from monkfish to squid, from sea urchins to scampi.

Fish is good for you. It's filled with vitamins, minerals and protein. And it's low in harmful fats. In fact, recent medical studies indicate that some fish—the so-called "oily" ones, such as salmon, tuna, swordfish, etc.—play a role in reducing cholesterol in the human body, thus lessening the chance of heart disease. And mollusks—clams, scallops, oysters and mussels—are among the richest sources of protein available.

Fish tastes good, too. Despite decades of overcooking, deep-frying and other less decorous maltreatment, fish—when properly prepared—is one of our most delicious of foods. Sautéed, broiled, braised, poached or baked, fish can never fail to suprise and delight with its delicate flavors and ever-varying textures.

When possible, always buy fresh fish. Freezing changes the texture and taste of fish more than almost any other food and, once thawed, frozen fish remain watery and lose their delicacy of flavor.

Freshness can be guaranteed by buying from a reputable fish dealer and knowing what to look for. Fish should be clear-eyed, fresh smelling and firm and always bedded in ice. Mollusks—clams, mussels and oysters (scallops are always sold already shelled in North America)—should be tightly shut, as clean as possible and uncracked. Crustaceans—crabs, lobsters, shrimp—should be firm, without any ammonia smell and, if alive, the tail or claws should be springy and snapping . . . watch out!

The most important thing to remember about cooking is that fish cooks fast. Allow a maximum of 10 minutes per inch of thickness. Thus, an average filet of sole will cook in 5–7 minutes. Shellfish is best boiled by a method I have worked out over the years. Fill a large pot with water and salt it generously. Add the shellfish and cover the pot. Bring to a rolling boil. Immediately remove from the heat and let sit, covered for a maximum of 10 minutes for lobsters and crabs, 1 minute for shrimp (this is not a misprint—

6

nothing is as awful as overcooked, mushy shrimp). Clams and mussels should be removed from the pot as soon as they open and need only a cup or two of liquid to cook.

In fact, all shellfish will preserve their flavor and texture better if steamed, using just enough liquid to make a depth of about 3/4-inch in the pot. The shellfish is not surrounded by water and the natural juices from the fish will not be diluted or leeched-out.

Whatever fish you cook, you can be sure of a healthful, light and tasty dish.

Baked Fish

One of the best ways to cook a whole fish, such as sea bass, lake trout, redfish, salmon or mackeral.

Butter or oil a large baking dish. Place the cleaned, scaled fish in the dish. Leave the head and tail on. The fish will be moister.

Sprinkle salt, pepper and bits of butter or a couple of spoonsful of oil over the fish. Bake in a 350 degree F. oven, allowing 10–12 minutes per inch of thickness (at the thickest part of the fish).

Variation: stuff the fish with slices of ripe tomato, peeled avocado and thinly sliced onion. Bake for an extra 5 minutes.

With wine and lemon: stuff the fish with 1 thinly sliced lemon. Sprinkle 2 tablespoons of dry white wine over the fish for each pound of cleaned weight.

Grilled Fish

An especially good way to cook fish steaks and fillets. Oil the broiler rack. Place the fish on the rack and brush with oil. Preheat the broiler and place the fish as close as possible to the heat. Broil for 7–10 minutes, depending on the thickness of the fish. Do not turn.

Variation: marinate the fish in olive oil, chopped garlic, black pepper and chopped fresh herbs (rosemary, tarragon and basil are good) for 1–2 hours before grilling.

8

Shrimp &
Three-Bean Salad

10 | Shrimp and Three-Bean Salad

1 cup drained cooked red kidney beans
1 cup drained cooked white beans
1 cup drained cooked string beans
1/2 green pepper, chopped
1/2 sweet red pepper chopped
2 teaspoons chopped onion
1 tablespoon chopped pimento
1 pound cooked shrimp, shelled and deveined
3 tablespoons lemon juice
3/4 cup olive oil
1/2 teaspoon cayenne pepper
salt and pepper to taste

If canned beans are used, drain and rinse well. In a mixing bowl combine the beans with the green and red pepper, onion, pimento and shrimp. Toss well and set aside.

In a tight-sealing jar, combine the lemon juice, olive oil, cayenne pepper and salt and pepper to taste. Shake vigorously to blend the ingredients. Pour over the salad, toss well and chill for 1 hour. Serves 4.

Stuffed Clams

24 medium-size clams, in shell
4 large mushrooms, chopped
2 shallots, chopped
2 tablespoons dry bread crumbs
6 tablespoons butter, softened
1 tablespoon chopped parsley
black pepper
1/3 cup grated Parmesan cheese
2 lemons, quartered

Carefully open the clam shells (or have the fish market do this) and remove the clams. Wash the shells and set aside.

Preheat the oven to 350 degrees F.

Rinse the clams and chop them.

In a large bowl combine the chopped clams with the mushrooms, shallots, bread crumbs, butter, parsley and pepper to taste.

Fill the clam shells with the mixture, sprinkle with Parmesan and place on a baking sheet. Bake for 15 minutes or until lightly browned and heated through. Transfer to a platter and surround with lemon wedges. Serves 4.

Lime-Walnut Salmon

rind of 1 lime, cut into julienne strips
7 tablespoons chilled sweet butter
4 8-ounce salmon steaks
2 tablespoons lime juice
3 tablespoons walnut oil
salt and pepper to taste
1 teaspoon finely chopped fresh mint

Preheat the oven to warm.

In a small saucepan, bring 1/2 cup of water to a boil. Add the lime rind and boil for 1 minute. Drain and let cool.

Melt 2 tablespoons of the butter in a large skillet. Put the salmon steaks into the skillet and let them cook over medium heat, turning once, until lightly browned, about 4 minutes per side. Transfer to a heat-proof platter and keep warm in the oven.

Add to the skillet the lime juice, lime rind, remaining butter and walnut oil. Cook over low heat, stirring, until the mixture has thickened. Season with salt and pepper to taste.

Spoon sauce over the steaks, sprinkle with mint and serve. Serves 4.

12

Stuffed Clams

14 | Shrimp Stir Fry

1 pound medium-size shrimp, shelled and deveined
3 tablespoons olive oil
1 tablespoon lemon juice
1 small green pepper, diced
1 small red pepper, diced
2 garlic cloves, finely chopped
1 large onion, coarsely chopped
2 large tomatoes, seeded and coarsely chopped
2 small zucchini, thinly sliced
1 teaspoon Tabasco
salt and pepper to taste

Heat the olive oil in a large skillet. Add the lemon juice, green and red peppers and cook, stirring constantly, over medium heat for three minutes. Add the zucchini, tomatoes, Tabasco and salt and pepper to taste. Stir well, cover the skillet and simmer for 5 minutes.

Add shrimp to the vegetables and stir well. Cover the skillet and simmer for 5 minutes longer. Serve over rice. Serves 4.

Crab Casserole

3 pounds crab legs
8 tablespoons butter
1 1/2 cups coarse cracker crumbs
2 large onions, finely chopped
6 celery stalks, finely chopped
2 tablespoons finely chopped parsley
1/4 cup heavy cream
1/2 teaspoon cayenne pepper
1 1/2 teaspoons dry mustard

Rinse the crab legs. Place in a steamer and steam for 10 minutes. Drain, shell and remove any cartilage from the meat. Break up the crab meat and place in a large bowl.

Preheat the oven to 350 degrees F. Grease a medium-size casserole with butter.

In a small saucepan melt the butter over low heat. Remove from heat and set aside to cool.

Add the cracker crumbs, onions, celery and parsley to the crab meat and mix well.

In a small bowl combine the cooled melted butter, cream, cayenne pepper and dry mustard. Mix well.

Add the cream mixture to the crab meat mixture and mix well. Spoon the mixture into the casserole and bake for 30 minutes. Serves 4.

Fish Kabobs

16 jumbo shrimp, shelled and deveined
1 lobster tail, shelled and cut into 4 chunks
8 sea scallops
8 large mushrooms
8 sweet red pepper chunks
6 tablespoons olive oil
2 tablespoons lemon juice
1 teaspoon oregano
1/2 teaspoon salt
1/2 teaspoon black pepper
1/2 teaspoon cayenne pepper

Spear the shrimp, lobster, scallops and red pepper chunks equally on 4 metal skewers.

Preheat the broiler. Heat the olive oil in a small saucepan and blend in the lemon juice, oregano, salt and pepper and cayenne pepper. Place the kabobs on a rack in the broiler pan and brush them with the oil mixture. Broil for 8 minutes, turning often and brushing with the oil each time.

These kabobs can also be marinated in the mixture first, then broiled, or they can be grilled over charcoal. Serve with rice or pilaf. Serves 4.

16

Shrimp Stir Fry

18 | Baked Oysters

24 large oysters
3 tablespoons butter
1 tablespoon lemon juice
1 tablespoon fresh basil leaves, finely chopped
black pepper to taste

Preheat the oven to 375 degrees F.

Scrub, rinse and dry the oysters. Place them on a baking sheet and bake for 3 minutes or until they open.

While the oysters are baking, in a small saucepan melt the butter. Blend in the lemon juice, basil and black pepper to taste.

Remove the oysters from the oven. Remove and discard the upper shells. Baste the oysters with the butter mixture, return to the oven and bake for 3 minutes. Serve immediately. Serves 4.

Stuffed Mackerel

2 mackerel, about 1 1/2 pounds each
1/2 pound cranberries
5 tablespoons bread crumbs
5 tablespoons butter, softened
1 tablespoon lemon juice
1 tablespoon dry sherry
1 teaspoon anchovy paste
salt and pepper to taste

Clean the mackerel. Remove the heads and tails, split the fish down the spine and remove the bones. Set aside. Preheat the oven to 375 degrees F. Lightly butter a baking dish large enough to hold both fish.

Chop the cranberries coarsely. In a mixing bowl combine the cranberries with the bread crumbs, butter, lemon juice, sherry, anchovy paste and salt and pepper to taste.

Stuff each mackerel with half the berry mixture. Wrap each fish in aluminum foil. Place the fish parcels in the baking dish and bake for 30 minutes. The parcels can also be placed over a charcoal fire and cooked as is. Serves 4.

Cod in Lemon-Butter

4 8-ounce cod fillets
6 tablespoons butter, melted
4 tablespoons lemon juice
1 teaspoon garlic, chopped
2 tablespoons fresh bread crumbs
salt and pepper to taste

Preheat the broiler.

In a shallow, oven proof baking dish, combine the butter, lemon juice, garlic, salt and pepper. Turn the fillets in the dish to coat them well with the mixture.

Place the baking dish under the broiler and cook for 5 minutes. Turn the fillets, sprinkle with the bread crumbs and return to the broiler for 5 minutes more. Transfer to a serving platter, pour over the pan juices and serve. Serves 4.

Fish Baked with Pine Nuts

2 whole firm fish, about 1 1/2 pounds each (use bass, trout, mullet)
4 tablespoons butter
2 cloves garlic, finely chopped
1/2 cup medium dry white wine (sauvignon blanc is ideal)
1/2 cup pine nuts, lightly toasted
salt and pepper to taste

Clean the fish, leaving the heads and tails on (they stay moister this way). Grease an oven proof baking dish with 1 tablespoon butter. Place a tablespoon of butter and 1 clove of the chopped garlic in the cavity of each fish, the remaining tablespoon of butter cut up and scattered over the tops of the fish. Season with salt and pepper.

Place in a 400 degree F. oven for 5 minutes.

Remove from the oven and pour over the wine. Return to a 350 degree F. oven for 10 minutes, until the wine is reduced and the fish is browned. Remove to a serving platter, pour the sauce around the fish and scatter the pine nuts over the fish. Serves 4.

Fish Kabobs

22 | Aioli-Walnut Fish Steaks

Aioli is the garlic mayonnaise of Provence. It is rich and wickedly garlicky.

For the fish:
4 fish steaks
1 onion, sliced
2 slices lemon
1 stick celery
1/2 teaspoons black peppercorns, roughly crushed
1 cup dry white wine

FOR THE AIOLI
5-6 cloves of garlic, peeled and crushed
2 egg yolks, at room temperature
1 cup extra virgin olive oil
1 tablespoon lemon juice
1/4 cup walnuts, roughly chopped

In a deep skillet place the onion, celery, peppercorns, white wine and enough water to cover the fish steaks. Bring to a boil and simmer for 20 minutes. Strain and return the liquid to the pan. Place the fish steaks in the bouillon and poach gently for 10 minutes, until cooked through. Lift out carefully and arrange on a platter.

While the fish is poaching, place the garlic and egg yolks in the bowl of a food processor and process for 5 seconds. Gradually add the oil with the processor on low, drop-by-drop at first, then in a steady stream as the mass thickens. When the oil is all used up, add the lemon juice and blend well.

Place the hot fish steaks on a platter, spread equal portions of the aioli on top of each steak and top with the chopped walnuts. Serve immediately. Serves 4.

Shrimp in Beer

3 cups beer
2 cloves garlic, chopped
1 teaspoon celery seed
2 tablespoons finely chopped parsley
1 teaspoon Tabasco sauce
3 tablespoons lemon juice
salt and pepper to taste
2 pounds medium shrimp, shelled and deveined
8 tablespoons butter (1 stick)

In a large saucepan combine the beer, garlic, celery seed, parsley, Tabasco sauce, lemon juice and salt and pepper to taste. Bring to a boil over medium heat.

When the beer is at a full boil, add the shrimp. When it returns to a boil, reduce the heat and simmer for 3 minutes.

Melt the butter in a small saucepan. Keep warm.

Drain the shrimp and transfer to a serving bowl. Pour the melted butter into individual dipping bowls. Serve immediately. Serves 4.

Baked Oysters

Barbecued Halibut

4 8-ounce halibut steaks
1/3 cup brandy
1/3 cup lemon juice
1/2 teaspoon dried dill
1 bay leaf
1 medium-size red onion, thinly sliced
1/2 lemon thinly sliced
1/3 cup chili sauce
2 tablespoons melted butter

Combine brandy, lemon juice, dill and bay leaf in a shallow bowl. Add the fish steaks and top with the onion and lemon slices. Let marinate for 1 hour.

Drain the steaks, reserving the marinade. Discard the onion and lemon slices. Place the steaks on a well-oiled grill over hot coals.

Combine the reserved marinade with the chili sauce and butter. Baste the steaks every 2 minutes as they cook. Grill for 5-6 minutes per side. Serves 4.

New England Clam Chowder

24 clams
1/2 pound salt pork (or mild bacon), diced
3 onions, finely chopped
2 cups boiling water
2 tablespoons lemon juice
3 potatoes, peeled and diced
3 cups milk
2 cups heavy cream
1 teaspoon salt
2 teaspoons black pepper

Scrub the clams, open and remove, reserving the clam liquor. Chop the clams.

In a large pot, cook the salt pork or bacon over high heat,

stirring constantly, for 10 minutes, until lightly browned. Pour off most of the fat, add the onions and cook over medium heat for another 10 minutes.

Add the boiling water, lemon juice, potatoes, salt and pepper. Cover and simmer for 10 minutes. Add the reserved clam liquor and simmer for 10 minutes.

Add the clams, milk and cream. Simmer for 15 minutes, stirring frequently. Do not let the soup boil or the cream may curdle. Serves 6.

Shrimp Cocktail

24 large to jumbo shrimp
1 cup dry white wine
1 bay leaf
1/2 teaspoon roughly cracked black pepper

Shell and devein the shrimp. Place in a saucepan with the white wine, bay leaf and cracked pepper. Cover the pan, bring to a boil and turn off the heat, leaving the pan covered for 3 minutes. Drain the shrimp and keep at room temperature. Serve with this sauce, instead of the usual red horror:

1/2 cup extra virgin olive oil
2 tablespoons lemon juice
2 teaspoons Dijon mustard
salt and pepper to taste

Place all ingredients in a small jar and cap tightly. Shake vigorously until well blended and serve in small dishes for dipping the shrimp. Serves 4.

29

Stuffed Mackerel

30 Italian Seafood Salad

1 pound medium shrimp
1/2 pound small squid
2 pounds mussels
1 large onion, chopped
2 cloves garlic, chopped
1 red pepper, peeled, seeded and chopped
1 stalk celery, finely sliced
3/4 cup extra virgin olive oil
4 tablespoons lemon juice
1/2 cup chopped basil leaves
salt and pepper to taste

Peel and devein the shrimp. Wash the squid and cut into 1/4-inch wide rings. Scrub the mussels. In a large saucepan, place the shrimp and squid with 2 cups water. Bring to a boil, cover and let sit off the heat for 3 minutes. Drain and place the shrimp and squid in a mixing bowl. In the same pot place the mussels with another 2 cups of water. Cover and bring to a boil, stirring frequently and removing the mussels as they open. Drain and when cool enough to handle, shell the mussels and add them to the mixing bowl.

In a separate bowl mix all the other ingredients well with a fork or whisk. Pour over the seafood and toss well. Let stand for 1 hour. Serves 4.

Crab Cakes

2 pounds crab legs
4 tablespoons butter
2 medium onions, finely chopped
1 cup soft unflavored bread crumbs
1 teaspoon dry mustard
1 teaspoon Worcestershire sauce
2 tablespoons light cream
1/2 cup flour
1 cup olive oil
salt

In a pot bring 2 quarts of water to a boil over a high heat. Add the crab legs. When the water returns to a boil, reduce the heat. Simmer the legs for 15 minutes. Drain the crab legs, shell them, and remove the cartilage. Flake the meat into a large bowl.

In a large skillet, melt the butter. Add the onions and cook over a low heat until they are soft but not brown. Pour the contents of the skillet over the crab meat. Add the bread crumbs and mix thoroughly.

In a small bowl beat the eggs. Add the mustard, Worcestershire sauce and a pinch of salt. Mix well and add to the crab mixture. Then add the creamed mix thoroughly.

Shape the crab mixture into 12 cakes. Put the flour on a plate. Dredge cakes in the flour.

Heat the olive oil in a large skillet. When the oil is hot, add the cakes. Fry until they are golden brown, about 3 minutes. Carefully turn the crab cakes and cook the other sides until brown. Serve with lemon or lime if desired. Serves 6.

Sautéed Soft-Shell Crabs

12 soft-shell crabs
flour
1 tablespoon ground ginger
1 tablespoon ground coriander
butter
salt to taste
black pepper to taste

Rinse the crabs thoroughly and drain well. Fill a small plastic or paper bag one-quarter filled with flour. Add the ginger and coriander, mix well. Put the crabs into the bag, one at a time, and shake until they are well coated with flour.

Melt enough butter in a skillet to fill it to a depth of 1/2 inch. Heat the butter until it bubbles. Add as many crabs to the skillet as will fit without the crabs touching each other. Dust the top of the crabs with salt and pepper and fry until the crabs are golden brown on the bottom. Turn the crabs over, dust again with salt and pepper, and fry until golden. Continue this procedure until all the crabs are fried, adding more butter as needed.

Serve the crabs hot with the butter and drippings spooned over them. Garnish with lemons if desired. Serves 6.

Aioli-Walnut
Fish Steaks

33

34 | Pecan-Coated Mako

4 8-ounce mako steaks
1 teaspoon salt
2 teaspoons black pepper
4 tablespoons flour
5 tablespoons butter
4 tablespoons olive oil
2 tablespoons lemon or lime juice
1/2 cup pecan halves
2 celery stalks, peeled and slivered
1 sweet red pepper, slivered

Wash and dry the mako steaks. Preheat the oven to 250 degrees F.

On a plate, combine the salt and pepper with the flour.

In a large skillet, melt 2 tablespoons of the butter and the olive oil over a low heat.

While the oil is heating, rub the steaks with the lemon or lime juice. Dredge each steak in the flour, shake off the excess and put it in the skillet. Cook the steaks for 5 minutes on each side. Drain them well on paper towels. Gently pat the steaks dry with additional towels, then transfer them to a serving platter. Place the platter in the oven. To the same skillet, add the remaining butter, the pecan halves, celery, and red pepper. Cook over a medium heat for 8 minutes, stirring constantly.

Remove the platter from the oven and using a slotted spoon, cover the mako with the pecan and vegetable mixture. Serves 4.

Seviche

2 pounds fresh firm white fish steaks or scallops
juice of 3 limes
juice of 3 lemons
1 large sweet red pepper
1 large red onion, thinly sliced and separated into rings
1 cup chopped scallions (green part only)
3/4 cup olive oil
salt to taste
black pepper to taste

Slice the fish into strips approximately 4 x 1/2 inch in size. Put the strips into a shallow dish and cover with the lime and lemon juice. Mix well, cover, and refrigerate for 4 hours.

Place the red peppers on a broiler pan and broil, turning often, until the pepper is blackened all over. Put the pepper into a paper bag and fold the bag closed. Let the pepper cool for 8 to 10 minutes. Remove it from the bag and rub off the skin, using your fingers. Seed and stem the pepper and cut it into thin strips.

Remove the fish from the refrigerator and discard the marinade. In a bowl (preferably glass) make layers of the fish, red onions, red pepper strips and chopped scallion. Salt and pepper each layer heavily.

Pour the olive oil over the bowl, cover, and chill. Serve as an appetizer or first course with thinly sliced bread. Serves 8.

Lobster Bisque

2 cups milk
2 cups heavy cream
4 tablespoons butter
1 large onion, finely chopped
2 tablespoons flour
1/2 teaspoon sweet paprika
1 teaspoon salt
1/2 teaspoon black pepper
2 cups cooked lobster meat
1 teaspoon lemon juice
1/4 cup dry sherry

In a large bowl, whisk together the milk and cream. Set aside.

In a large saucepan melt the butter. Add the onion. Cook over medium heat, stirring constantly, for 5 minutes, or until the vegetables are tender, but not brown. Stir in the flour, paprika, salt and pepper. Still stirring, pour the milk and cream together into the saucepan in a slow but steady stream. Quickly bring the sauce to a boil. Stir constantly to make sure the soup is smooth. Reduce the heat and simmer for 3 minutes.

Put the lobster meat into a bowl. Add the lemon juice and mix well. Add the lobster to the soup. Stir in the sherry. Simmer the soup for 5 more minutes stirring frequently. Pour the soup into serving bowls and serve immediately. Serves 6.

Fish Baked
with Pine Nuts

38 | Shrimp & Corn Chowder

3 tablespoons butter
1/4 cup chopped scallions
1 garlic clove, finely chopped
1/2 teaspoon black pepper
1 1/2 cups light cream
1/2 cup water
2 potatoes, peeled and diced
1/4 teaspoon salt
1/2 teaspoon dried parsley
2 cups milk
3 ounces cream cheese
1 cup whole kernel corn, drained
1 1/2 pounds shrimp, shelled, deveined and chopped

Melt the butter in a large heavy pot. Add the scallions, garlic and pepper and sauté over low heat until the scallions are tender but not browned.

Add the cream, water, potatoes, salt, parsley and milk. Simmer for 15 to 20 minutes, or until the potatoes are soft. Stir frequently so the cream and milk do not form a skin. Do not allow the mixture to come to a boil.

Soften the cream cheese with a fork, then stir it into the soup. When the cream cheese is fully blended, add the corn and shrimp. Bring the soup slowly to a boil, then immediately reduce the heat and simmer for 5-10 minutes or until the shrimp are white and tender. Serve the chowder piping. Serves 6.

Spicy Red Snapper

4 8-ounce red snapper fillets
2 tablespoons olive oil
1 garlic clove, finely chopped
1 large onion, chopped
1/2 cup pimento-stuffed green olives, sliced
1/2 small sweet red pepper, chopped
1 teaspoon ground cumin
1 teaspoon chili powder
1 dried hot red chili, finely chopped
6 tablespoons lemon juice
6 tablespoons orange juice
salt and pepper to taste

Wash and dry the fillets. Put the fillets into a lightly buttered baking dish. Preheat the oven to 375 degrees F.

In a large skillet over medium-low heat, heat the olive oil. Add the garlic and chopped onion. Cook, stirring constantly until the onion is soft. Add the sliced olives, sweet red pepper and mix well. Add the lemon juice, orange juice and salt and pepper to taste and stir until well blended. Simmer for 5 minutes.

Pour the sauce over the fish. Bake uncovered for 20 minutes. Carefully transfer the fillets to a serving platter. Pour the sauce over them and serve. Serves 4.

40

New England
Clam Chowder

42 | Shrimp Jambalaya

5 tablespoons of butter
3 tablespoons of flour
1 large sweet white onion
2 cloves of garlic, finely chopped
2 cups Italian plum tomatoes
1/2 cup cubed slab bacon
2 tablespoons chopped fresh parsley
1 teaspoon crushed red pepper flakes
2 red bell peppers, chopped
2 cups long grain white rice
2 cups chicken broth, heated
1 cup clam juice, heated
2 1/2 pounds medium shrimp, shelled, deveined and cleaned
salt, to taste
black pepper, to taste

In a large skillet melt the butter, then add the flour. Stir well.
Cook, stirring constantly, over a low heat for approximately
3 minutes. Add the onion and chopped garlic and continue cooking over a medium heat until the onions begin to soften.

   Add the tomatoes and bacon and cook for 2-3 more minutes.
Add the parsley, salt, pepper, crushed red pepper flakes, tomatoes
and the rice. Add the broth and clam juice to the skillet. The
mixture should be totally covered, add more liquid if necessary.
Cover the pan and simmer over a low heat for approximately
25 minutes, or until the rice is tender.

   Add the shrimp at the last minute and cook with the mixture.
The shrimp should not need more than 5 minutes, maybe less.
Serves 6.

Boiled Lobster

4 lobsters
1/2 cup butter, melted
1 lemon, cut in quarters
salt

In a large heavy pot boil enough water so that the lobsters will be completely covered when they are added. Add 1 tablespoon of salt for each quart of water you use. Bring the water to a boil and place the lobsters in, head first.

Quickly, bring the water back to the boil and then reduce the heat to simmer. Cook the lobsters approximately 3-4 minutes per pound.

Serve the lobsters whole with the melted butter and lemon. Serves 4.

Paupiettes of Sole

4 thick fillets of sole
1/2 cup dry white wine
4 tablespoons of dry white wine
1/2 cup thinly sliced scallions
1 peeled and thinly sliced carrot
1/2 cup thinly sliced red onion
1/2 cup finely chopped basil
black pepper to taste

Preheat the oven to 350 degrees F.

Put the fish in a bowl. Pour the wine over fish and allow this to marinate while you prepare the rest of the dish. Turn occasionally.

In a heavy skillet melt the butter over a medium heat. Add the scallions, carrots and onion. Cook, stirring occasionally, until soft, approximately 5 minutes. Remove the skillet from the heat

Place four large pieces of parchment or aluminum foil on a working surface. The pieces should be large enough to go around the fillets twice.

Place one teaspoon of liquid from the skillet in the center of each piece of foil. Top each with a fish fillet, one-quarter of the vegetable mixture and the basil. Pour one-quarter of the remaining wine over each piece of fish and top with any remaining liquid from the skillet.

Fold the edges of the foil tightly together to make a heavy leak-proof seam. It is easiest to fold the long seam first and then the edges.

Place the packets on a baking sheet and bake in the oven for 20-30 minutes. When ready to serve, open the packets with a sharp knife or scissors. Serves 4.

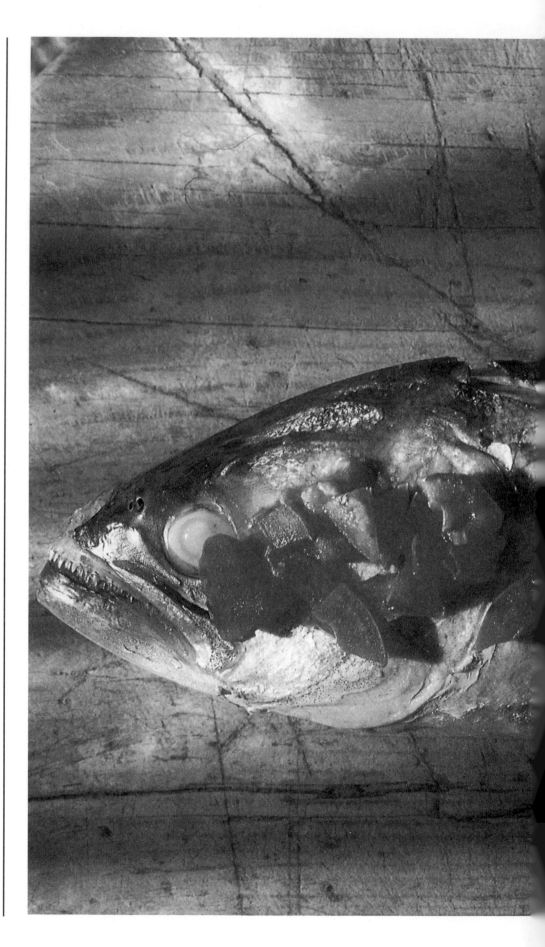

Bluefish with
Tomato Concassé

45

Mussels with White Wine

1/2 cup butter
6 shallots, chopped
1 clove of garlic, chopped
1/2 cup dry white wine
black pepper
6 pounds of mussels, scrubbed, bearded and cleaned
1/2 cup chopped parsley

In a small skillet melt the butter over a medium heat. Add the shallots and garlic. Cook, stirring occasionally for 2-3 minutes.

In a large heavy pot heat the wine. Add the shallot mixture. Stir. Add the mussels and stir. Cover tightly and cook over a high heat for 6-8 minutes, shaking the pan or stirring the mussels to ensure even heat. Remove the mussels as soon as they open and place in a serving bowl. Pour the cooking liquid over the mussels and serve while hot. Serves 4.

Bluefish with Tomato Concassé

6 8-ounce bluefish fillets
2 tablespoons butter, melted
2 tablespoons olive oil
2 tablespoons lemon juice
1 tablespoon Worcestershire sauce
1 tablespoon red wine vinegar
1 teaspoon finely chopped parsley
1 scallion, finely chopped
3 tomatoes, coarsely chopped
salt to taste
black pepper to taste

Wash and dry the fillets. Place them on the rack of a large broiler pan. Preheat the broiler.

In a small bowl, combine the melted butter and olive oil. Brush the top of the fillets with the mixture. Cook the fillets for 8-10 minutes on the first side.

While the fillets are broiling, combine in a small saucepan the lemon juice, Worcestershire sauce, red wine vinegar, parsley, scallion and tomatoes. Salt and pepper to taste.

Remove the pan from the broiler, baste with the sauce and broil for 2 minutes longer.

Turn the fish and baste with the sauce. Return to the broiler and cook for 5 more minutes. While the fish is in the broiler, heat the remaining sauce over a low heat.

Transfer the fillets to a serving platter and pour the sauce over them. Serves 6.

Monkfish-Grapefruit Salad

1 pound monkfish
1/2 grapefruit, peeled and broken into sections
1/2 cup black or green olives
1/2 cup olive oil
2 tablespoons red wine or balsamic vinegar
1 teaspoon Dijon-style mustard
salt to taste
black pepper to taste

Place the monkfish in a saucepan and fill with enough cold water to cover. With the cover on, bring the water to the boil. Once it has boiled, remove from the heat and let stand covered for 5 minutes. Allow the fish to cool thoroughly before using.

Thinly slice the cooled fish and chill for approximately 30 minutes.

In a serving bowl combine the fish with the olives and grapefruit sections.

In a small bowl combine the olive oil, vinegar, mustard and salt and pepper. Mix well. Pour over the salad. Toss and serve.
Serves 4.

48

Shrimp in Beer

Crab Cakes

50 | Seafood Pasta Salad

1 pound of small pasta shells or ziti
1/2 cup plus 2 tablespoons of olive oil
1/2 pound snow peas, trimmed
1 sweet red pepper, thinly sliced
1 pound cooked shrimp, shelled and deveined
1/2 pound cooked crab meat, flaked
1/2 pound bay scallops or sea scallops, quartered
1 small red onion, thinly sliced
1 cup pitted whole black olives
1 1/2 teaspoons dried dill
2 garlic cloves, finely chopped
1/2 cup lemon juice
salt to taste
black pepper to taste

Cook the pasta in salted boiling water. When the pasta is almost done, add the snow peas and the red pepper. Cook for 2 minutes. Drain well.

Put the pasta mixture into a serving bowl. Add the 2 tablespoons of olive oil and toss well.

Add to the pasta mixture the shrimp, crabmeat and scallops, red onion and olives. Mix thoroughly.

In a small bowl combine the dill, garlic, lemon juice, 1/2 cup of olive oil and salt and pepper to taste. Mix well. When the dressing is blended, pour it over the seafood mixture. Toss gently but thoroughly. Serves 6.

Italian Fish Stew

18 clams in shells
2 pounds sea bass fillets
1 pound shrimp, peeled and deveined
1 large lobster tail, shelled and deveined
1 pound crab legs, shelled and cartilage removed
1/2 cup olive oil
1 large onion, chopped
1 green pepper, chopped
1 sweet red pepper, chopped
12 straw mushrooms
4 ripe tomatoes, peeled and chopped
4 garlic cloves, finely chopped
1/2 cup tomato purée
1 cup red wine
1 cup dry sherry
small bunch parsley, chopped
1 teaspoon sugar (or to taste)
1/2 teaspoon crushed red pepper
1 tablespoon oregano
salt to taste
pepper to taste

Scrub the clams and set aside. Cut the sea bass fillets into serving size pieces. Cut the lobster tail and the crab legs into pieces. Put the bass, lobster, crab and shrimp into a large pot. Set aside.

In a large skillet, heat the olive oil. Add the onion, red pepper, green pepper, garlic and mushrooms. Cook over a low heat for 5 minutes, stirring frequently. Add the tomatoes, tomato purée, red wine, sugar, sherry, half the parsley, red pepper, oregano, and salt and pepper to taste. Cover the skillet and cook over a low heat for 15 minutes. Carefully pour the sauce and vegetables into the pot with the fish. Mix well and cook gently for 30 minutes.

Add the clams and continue to simmer until the clams open. Transfer the stew to a large serving bowl. Sprinkle with the remaining parsley and serve. Serves 6.

53

Italian Seafood Salad

Seafood Crêpes

1 pound cooked seafood (include any assortment of the
  following: shrimp, scallops, lobster and crab)
2 ounces drained anchovies
2 tablespoons chopped basil
1/2 teaspoon salt
6 eggs, beaten
1 cup flour
1 cup cold water
2 teaspoons finely chopped onion
2 tablespoons oil or butter

Cut the seafood into bite-size pieces. In a medium-sized mixing bowl, combine the seafood, anchovies, basil, salt and pepper. Mix well.

In another mixing bowl, combine the eggs, flour, water and onions. Mix thoroughly to form the batter.

Lightly grease a large skillet with the oil or melt the butter. Ladle 3 tablespoons of the batter at a time into the skillet, spreading it evenly. Cook for 3-5 minutes, or until the crêpe is solid but still slightly moist. Carefully remove the crêpe to plate. Repeat this process until all the crêpes are made.

Evenly divide the filling among the 6 crêpes. Fold the crêpe over and set aside on a large baking sheet.

Preheat the oven to 450 degrees F.

Place the baking sheet in the oven and bake for 8 minutes. Serves 6.

Scampi

One of the most abused words in the Italian language. Scampi are really a variety of shellfish known as Norway lobsters or Dublin Bay prawns. They are only obtainable in this country frozen and are very expensive indeed. However, the word has come to mean any large shrimp prepared with a high dosage of garlic.

2 pounds jumbo shrimp in their shells
4 tablespoons butter
4 tablespoons olive oil
4 cloves garlic, finely chopped
2 tablespoons fresh parsley, finely chopped
2 lemons, cut in half

Wash the shrimp. Cut them down their undersides but not quite all the way through—butterflied, in fact. Flatten them slightly with a rolling pin or bottle. Melt the butter in a small saucepan, add the olive oil, garlic and mix well. Remove from the heat. Place the scampi, shell side facing up, on a rack in a broiling pan. Paint the shells with half the butter-oil-garlic mixture. Preheat the broiler.

Broil the shrimp 6 inches from the heat for 3 minutes. Remove the pan and turn the shrimp, paint them with the remaining mixture and return to the broiler for another 3 minutes. Serve immediately with chopped parsley sprinkled over them and perhaps a half lemon per person. Serves 4.

Smoked Fish Platter

Smoked fish is one of the world's great delicacies. All sorts of fish are smoked: trout, salmon, whitefish, sable, sturgeon, herrings, tuna, swordfish, mackerel, cod and eel are the most common. Don't be put off by eel. It is firm, sweet-tasting and boneless.

All are best served simply, filleted, with a green or mixed vegetable salad with lemon in the dressing rather than vinegar. An alternative is a horseradish-cream dressing. This is made by combining 1 tablespoon of grated horseradish to each 1/4 cup heavy cream. Or you can fold the horseradish into lightly whipped cream, for a lighter version.

If possible, buy a variety of different smoked fish and serve as a light lunch or as the first course to a dinner.

Shrimp Jambalaya

Boiled Lobster

58 | Paella

There are countless versions of this Spanish dish, but all have these ingredients in common: chicken, shellfish, rice and saffron. Sometimes sausage or pork is added and a variety of vegetables can be used, especially asparagus, artichoke hearts, fresh peas or string beans. Following is the basic, authentic method.

4 tablespoons olive oil
2 cloves garlic, roughly chopped
1 1/2 pounds chicken parts, cut into 8 pieces
2 cups long-grain rice
2 tomatoes, peeled and chopped
1 teaspoon paprika
1/2 pound medium shrimp, shelled and deveined
1/4 pound string beans
1/2 teaspoon saffron
salt and pepper to taste

In a very large—12-inch minimum— skillet or paella pan heat the olive oil over a medium flame. Add the garlic and let brown very lightly. Now add the chicken, skin side down and let cook gently for about 10 minutes. Remove and keep warm. Add the tomatoes to the pan and stir in the paprika. Add 6 cups of water. When it starts to bubble add the chicken pieces and cook for 10 minutes. Add the rice, shrimp and the string beans. Cook for 15 minutes and sprinkle in the saffron. If the water dries up before the rice is done add more by the half-cup. If the rice doesn't absorb it all, turn up the heat, stirring carefully. The rice should be moist and each grain separate. Salt and pepper to taste. Serves 4.

Grilled Herbed Sea Bass

6 8-ounce sea bass fillets
1 cup dry vermouth
1/3 cup olive oil
1 cup chopped fresh mushrooms
1/2 cup finely chopped onions
2 tablespoons lemon juice
2 teaspoons salt
1/2 teaspoon black pepper
1/4 teaspoon dried tarragon

Heat the coals in a barbecue until they are gray and very hot. Or preheat a gas grill to high.

Cut 6 pieces of heavy aluminum foil into large squares. Lightly oil the foil.

In a large bowl combine the vermouth, olive oil, mushrooms, onions, lemon juice, salt, pepper and tarragon. Mix well.

Place one fillet on each piece of foil. Evenly pour the dressing over each piece of fish. Wrap the fish carefully. Place the packages on the grill.

Grill for 20 minutes or until the fish flakes when tested with a fork or knife. Serves 6.

Mussels in White Wine

Seviche

62 | Barbecued Fish Steaks

The key to successful fish grilling is firm fish and marination to keep them moist and to prevent the fish from sticking to the grill. It's also a good idea to coat the grill surface with a spray cooking oil, such as Pam, before you start the fire. If you spray after the grill is hot, you will see a remarkable sheet of flame that might just singe your eyebrows.

2 pounds salmon or swordfish steaks
1/4 cup olive oil
1 lime
1 lemon
2 cloves garlic, chopped
1 tablespoon fresh basil, chopped
salt to taste
pepper to taste

In a shallow dish combine the olive oil, juice of the lime, lemon, garlic, basil salt and pepper. Mix to blend. Add the fish and coat well. Allow to marinate for at least 4 hours.

Prepare the grill. Remove the fish from the marinade and cook 4-8 minutes per side, turning only once. Brush with additional marinade while grilling, if desired. Cooking time will vary depending upon how well done you like your fish. Serves 4.

Shrimp Skewers

2 pounds large shrimp, peeled and deveined
1/2 cup olive oil
juice of 2 large lemons
2 cloves garlic, crushed
1 tablespoon chili powder
2 red bell peppers, cut into 1-1 1/2 inch pieces
1 yellow bell peppers, cut into 1-1 1/2 inch pieces
1 pound small mushrooms, whole or cut in half

In a large bowl, combine the olive oil, lemon juice, garlic and chili powder, mix well. Add the shrimp and coat thoroughly. Allow to marinate for 1 hour.

Arrange the shrimp, peppers and mushrooms on 6-8 skewers, beginning and ending with the shrimp. Reserve marinade for basting.

Prepare the grill. Place skewers on grill and cook for about 5-7 minutes, turning frequently and basting often. Carefully remove from skewers onto plates. Serves 4.

Grilled Fish Packets

4 thick firm fish filets (salmon, sole or flounder)
4 large pieces of aluminum foil
1/4 pound butter, melted
8 sprigs fresh thyme
8 sprigs fresh parsley
4 cloves garlic, coarsely chopped
salt to taste
black pepper to taste
4 tablespoons dry white wine
2 tablespoons butter, cut into 4 pieces

Place the pieces of foil on a working surface, shiny side face down. Brush the inside with the melted butter.

Place a fish filet on each piece of foil. Then evenly divide the thyme, parsley, garlic, salt, pepper and wine among the filets. Dot each filet with a piece of butter and then securely fold the foil and seal the edges.

Prepare the grill. Place packets on the grill and cook for 5-7 minutes. Place packets on plates and open carefully. Serves 4.

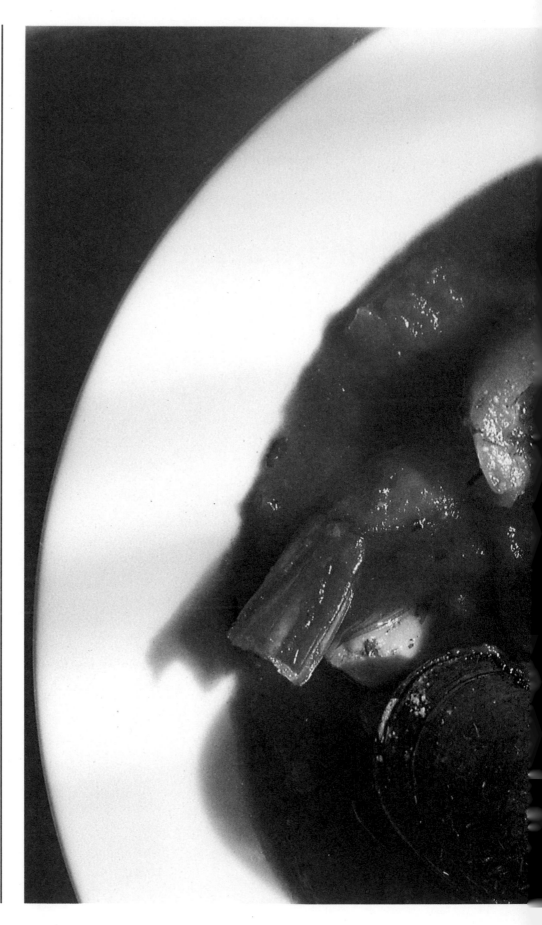

Italian Fish Stew

66 | Oysters on the Half-Shell

Again, a strike against the red menace! If you like oysters, there's no need to disguise their flavor. If you don't like oysters, read on.

For each serving:
6 oysters on the half-shell
6 halves lemon

Arrange each half-dozen oysters on a bed of ice in a shallow soup plate. Add lemon halves.

For those who wish a dipping sauce:
Combine, for each serving, 1/4 cup dry white wine, 1 teaspoon wine vinegar, 1/4 teaspoon freshly ground black pepper, 4-6 drops Tabasco sauce. Stir well.

Smoked Salmon Roll-Ups

1 cup soft herbed cream cheese
12 long, thin-cut slices smoked salmon
capers

Bring the cream cheese to room temperature.
   Place the salmon slices on a plate and spread evenly with the cream cheese. Roll up and secure with a toothpick if necessary. Garnish with capers. Serves 12.

Mussels Marinara

2 pounds mussels
1 onion, finely chopped
1 can imported Italian tomatoes, drained
1/2 cup parsley, chopped
black pepper
1-2 cups dry white wine

Scrub the mussels and remove the beards.

Place the mussels in a large pot and add the onions, tomatoes, parsley, pepper and wine. Cover and steam over medium heat until the mussels open.

Remove the mussels, with their shells, to a large serving bowl and cover with the liquid. Serve with crusty bread. Serves 4.

Shrimp Rémoulade

1 large onion, sliced
1 clove of garlic
2 pounds medium shrimp, cleaned and deveined
salt

RÉMOULADE
1 cup mayonnaise
1 tablespoon capers, chopped
2 teaspoons mustard
1 teaspoon tarragon
1 tablespoon drained mustard or cucumber pickle, finely chopped.

In a large pot combine the onion, garlic and salt, bring to a boil. Add the shrimp and simmer for 5 minutes or until just pink. Drain and chill.

Combine all the ingredients for the rémoulade in a small bowl. Chill.

When ready to serve, arrange the shrimp on small plates and top with a dollop of the sauce. Serves 6.

Scampi

Seafood Crêpes

70 | Stuffed Mussels

A middle eastern dish and an especially savory appetizer.

36 large mussels
1 small onion, peeled and finely chopped
3 tablespoons sesame oil
1 cup cooked long grain rice
3 tablespoons currants
2 tablespoons pine nuts
1/2 teaspoon ground coriander
1/2 teaspoon ground ginger
1/2 teaspoon black pepper
2 teaspoons sugar
lemon wedges

Clean and scrub the mussels. Place in a covered saucepan with 1 cup of water and bring to a boil. Cook, covered, until the mussels open. Drain and set aside.

Sauté the onion in the sesame oil until light golden. Add the rice and cook gently until lightly colored. Now add the currants, pine nuts, coriander, ginger, pepper and sugar. Cover the pan and simmer for 5 minutes.

Place a spoonful of the rice mixture into each mussel and close the shells. Serve at room temperature with lemon wedges.
Serves 6.

Seviche of Scallops

1 pound bay scallops
1 sweet onion, peeled and finely chopped
1 red pepper, peeled, seeded and chopped
1 yellow pepper, peeled, seeded and chopped
1 cup fresh lime juice
salt and pepper to taste

Combine all the ingredients in a china or glass bowl. Cover and chill for 2–3 hours. The lime juice "cooks" the fish. Serves 4.

Herring Salad

1 cup pickled herring, cubed
1 cup boiled potatoes, cubed
1/2 cup cooked beets, cubed
1 small onion, peeled and finely chopped
1/3 cup olive oil
1 tablespoon lemon juice
1 tablespoon fresh dill, chopped
salt and pepper to taste

Combine all the ingredients in a mixing bowl and toss well. Serve in mounds on salad plates with pumpernickel and sweet butter. Serves 4.

Salmon Mousse

2 1/2 teaspoons gelatin
2 tablespoons cold water
2 egg yolks
2 tablespoons sweet butter
1 1/4 teaspoons flour
1 teaspoon salt
1/2 teaspoon curry powder
1 teaspoon Dijon mustard
1 tablespoon lemon juice
3 tablespoons milk
1 1/2 cups cooked salmon, packed

Sprinkle the gelatin into the cold water, set aside.

In the top of a double boiler, over hot, not boiling water, combine the egg yolks, butter, flour, salt, curry powder, mustard, lemon juice and milk. Cook until the mixture begins to thicken. Add the gelatin and stir well. Chill.

Generously grease a ring mold. When the gelatin mixture is almost set, place some of it in the bottom of the mold and then top with the fish. Continue this until ingredients are finished, being sure to end with the gelatin mixture. Chill until firm. Unmold onto a serving plate. Serves 6.

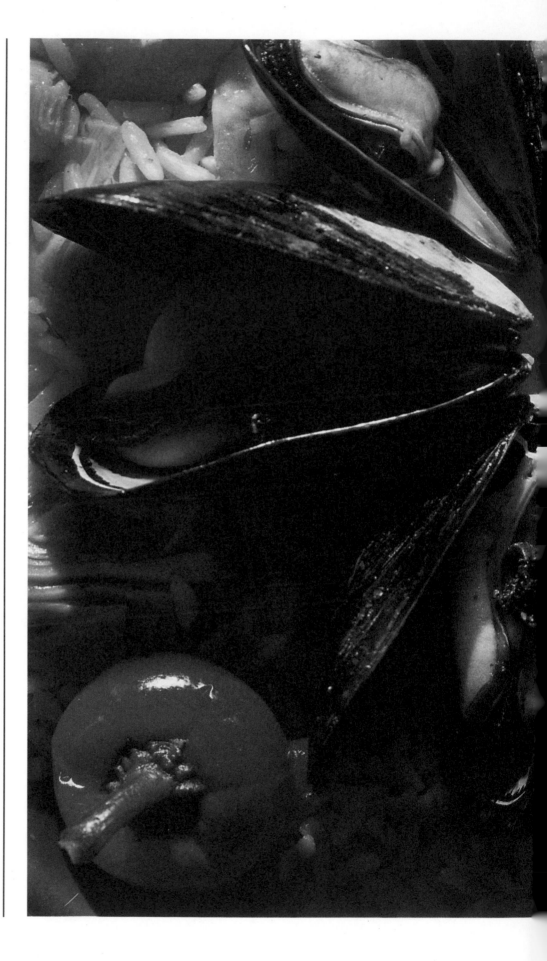

Paella

74 | Fresh Salmon Paté

1 pound fresh, boned salmon fillet
1 teaspoon salt substitute
1/2 teaspoon fresh peppercorns
2 tablespoons fresh lemon juice
1 tablespoon chopped fresh tarragon
1 small white onion
1 medium boiled potato, peeled and quartered
1 teaspoon fresh peppercorns
1/2 cup plain non-fat yogurt
non-fat crackers and toast points

Place the salmon fillet in a saucepan with water to cover, salt substitute and 1/2 teaspoon fresh peppercorns. Bring the mixture to a boil, lower the heat and cover and simmer for 15-20 minutes or until the salmon flakes easily. Let the salmon come to room temperature in the water. Drain, skin and flake.

In a food processor or blender combine the salmon, lemon juice, tarragon, onion, potato, fresh peppercorns and non-fat yogurt. Process until smooth. Transfer the mixture into a mold that has been sprayed with non-fat cooking spray or into ramekins. Cover and chill overnight. Serve surrounded with crackers and toast points. Serves 6 to 8.

Linguine with Tuna Sauce

1 tablespoon olive or vegetable oil
1 large white onion, chopped
2 cloves garlic, chopped
1/4 cup chopped fresh basil
1 large can Italian tuna in olive oil, drained
1 large can imported Italian plum tomatoes, drained
2-4 drops of Tabasco sauce
freshly ground pepper to taste
1 pound linguine

In a medium-size saucepan heat the oil, add the onion and garlic and cook only until wilted and translucent.

Add the basil, tuna and tomatoes to the saucepan, stir to combine. Season with Tabasco, pepper and cook over a low heat until sauce is hot and flavors are combined, approximately 15 minutes.

While the sauce is simmering, cook the pasta in a large pot of boiling water until it is *al dente*. Drain well.

Transfer the pasta to a large serving dish and spoon the sauce over the pasta. Toss gently but well. Serves 4.

Lime-Ginger Grilled Tuna

1/2 cup fresh lime juice
2 cloves fresh garlic, finely chopped
2 tablespoons olive oil
2 tablespoons vegetable oil
salt to taste, if desired
freshly ground black pepper to taste
1 1/2 teaspoons finely chopped fresh ginger
1 teaspoon slivered lime rind
6 fresh tuna steaks, about 1-inch thick

Combine the lime juice, garlic, olive oil, vegetable oil, salt , pepper, ginger and lime rind in a mixing bowl. Whisk until well blended.

Put the tuna steaks in a shallow dish large enough to hold them in one layer. Pour the marinade over the fish. Turn the steaks to coat well. Cover the dish and marinate in the refrigerator for 4 hours, turn occasionally.

Preheat the broiler or gas grill or prepare a charcoal grill.

Remove the tuna steaks from the marinade, reserve the marinade. Grill the steaks 3 inches from the heat until lightly browned, 3-5 minutes per side.

Put the reserved marinade into a saucepan and gently heat until hot.

Arrange steaks on a serving platter and pour hot marinade over each. Serves 6.

Fresh Salmon Paté

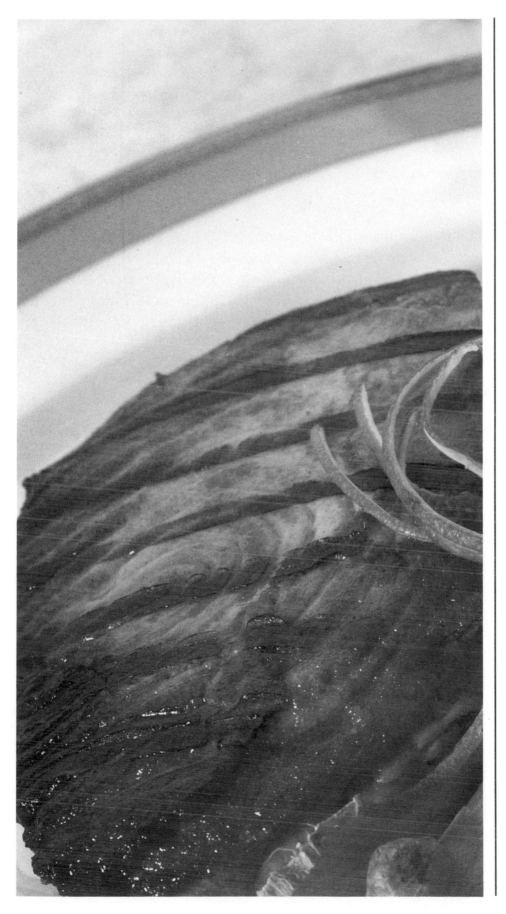

Lime-Ginger
Grilled Tuna

Spiced Broiled Salmon

1 tablespoon olive or vegetable oil
1 tablespoon Mongolian Fire oil or sesame oil
1 tablespoon dried orange peel
1/2 teaspoon coarsely ground black pepper
1 teaspoon chopped garlic in oil
2 pounds salmon fillet

In a shallow dish combine the olive oil, Mongolian Fire oil or sesame oil, dried orange peel, black pepper and garlic; stir to mix.

Cut the salmon fillet into 4 equal pieces. Place the fish, skin side up, into the marinade, turn to coat and then let marinate with the skin side up for at least 2 hours at room temperature.

Preheat the oven to broil. Lightly spray a broiling pan with low-calorie cooking spray. Place the fish, flesh side up, on the broiling pan. Broil gently for 10 to 15 minutes depending on the thickness of the fish. Do not turn. Fish will be charred and crispy outside, moist inside. Serves 4.

Grilled Marinated Swordfish

1/4 cup fresh lime juice
1/4 cup fresh lemon juice
1 teaspoon grainy mustard
1 clove of garlic, crushed
1/4 cup fresh tarragon, chopped
1/2 cup olive or vegetable oil
4 swordfish steaks, about 1 inch thick
coarsely ground black pepper

In a blender or in a jar combine the lime juice, lemon juice, mustard, garlic, tarragon and oil, process or shake until well mixed.

Place the swordfish steaks in a large shallow plate, pour the marinade over the steaks, turn to coat and season with black pepper. Cover and marinate for at least 2 hours, turning occasionally. Preheat the broiler or gas grill, or prepare a charcoal grill. Remove the steaks from the marinade. Grill the steaks 3 inches from the heat source for approximately 3-5 minutes per side or until done. Serves 4.

Gravlad Lax

2 pounds fresh salmon fillet
1/2 cup light brown sugar
2 tablespoons coarse salt
1 bunch fresh dill

Cut the fillet into two pieces. Spread the flesh sides with equal amounts of sugar, salt and chopped fresh dill. Sandwich the pieces together, flesh side to flesh side in a shallow dish. Cover with foil or plastic wrap. Place in the refrigerator and leave for 2-4 days.

Unwrap, separate the halves and cut in very thin slices, accompanied by buttered, thinly-sliced rye bread and mustard. Serves 8 as an appetizer.

Dilled Sea Scallops

3 tablespoons extra virgin olive oil
2 cloves garlic, finely chopped
1 pound sea scallops
1/2 cup dry white wine
1 tablespoon fresh dill weed, chopped

Sauté the garlic in the olive oil for 5 minutes. Add the dry scallops and cook until just heated through, about 5 minutes (if the scallops are very large, cut in half crosswise).

Add the white wine and dill and cook another 2 minutes. Serve over rice or pasta. Serves 4.

Grilled Marinated
Swordfish

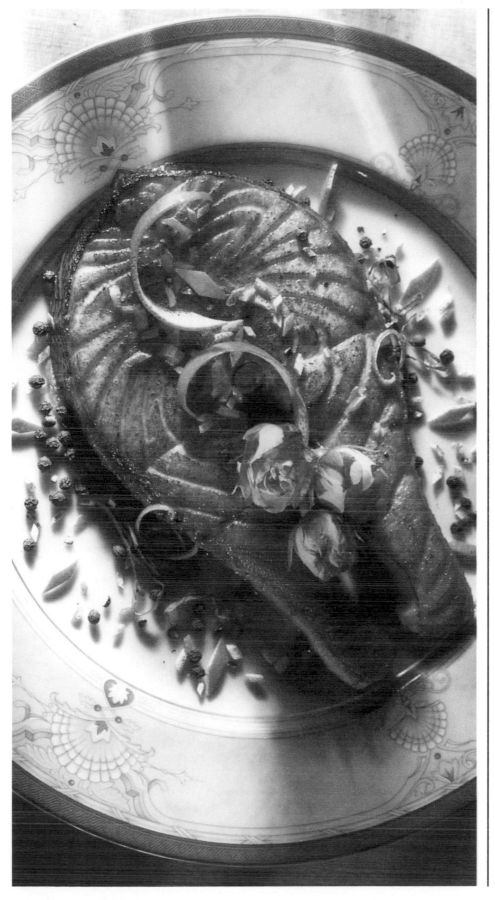

Spiced Broiled Salmon

82 | Shrimp & Fresh Coriander

2 pounds large shrimp, shelled and deveined
1/2 cup lime juice
1/4 cup sesame oil
2 tablespoons chopped fresh coriander
1 teaspoon black pepper
1 small chili pepper

Marinate the shrimp in the ingredients for 2 hours. Thread the shrimp on four skewers and grill or broil for no more than 5 minutes, turning several times. Serves 4.

Spicy Scallops with Curly Endive

1 clove garlic, chopped
1 large onion, peeled and finely chopped
1 sweet red pepper, peeled, seeded and julienned
2 tablespoons olive oil
1 pound sea scallops, halved if large
1 teaspoon Tabasco sauce
1 1/2 pounds curly endive, washed and coarsely shredded
2 tablespoons olive oil
freshly ground black pepper, to taste

In a large sauté pan, gently fry the garlic, onions and red pepper in the olive oil until soft, but not brown. Set aside. In the same pan, sauté the scallops over medium high heat until seared and just cooked through, about 4-5 minutes. Return the vegetable mixture to the pan and cover, off the heat.

Add the other 2 tablespoons of olive oil. Sauté the curly endive until limp and hot through. Arrange on a platter and top with the scallop-vegetable mixture. Season liberally with freshly ground black pepper. Serves 4.

Baked Whole Red Snapper

4-5 pound whole red snapper, split and cleaned
1 bunch scallions, finely chopped
1 teaspoon chopped garlic
1/2 teaspoon mixed peppercorns
1 cup sliced mushrooms
1 ripe tomato, coarsely chopped
1 teaspoon fresh thyme
2 tablespoons fresh lime juice
2 tablespoons low-fat margarine
freshly ground black pepper
1/2 cup white wine

Preheat the oven to 375 degrees F. Spray a roasting pan with low-calorie cooking spray; be sure the entire fish will fit in the pan.

Place the scallions, garlic, mixed peppercorns, mushrooms, tomatoes and thyme in the cavity of the fish. Sprinkle with lime juice and place 1 tablespoon of the margarine in the center. Skewer the fish closed.

Transfer the fish to the roasting pan. Cover the outside with freshly ground black pepper and place the remaining tablespoon of margarine on the top of the fish. Pour the wine over the fish.

Bake in the oven for 30-40 minutes or until firm. Baste every 10 minutes with pan juices. Serves 4.

Chilled Mussels
in Spicy Sauce

Warm Scallop Salad

86 | Grilled Skewered Sea Scallops

2 pounds sea scallops
3 tablespoons olive oil
1 tablespoon light soy sauce
1 tablespoon rice vinegar
1/2 cup chopped fresh cilantro
3 bell peppers; red, orange and yellow, cored,
   and sliced into chunks
1 yellow onion, coarsely chopped
1 box button mushrooms

In a large bowl, combine the olive oil, light soy sauce, rice vinegar and cilantro. Whisk to blend and add the sea scallops and turn several times until well coated. Allow mixture to marinate for 3 hours.

Preheat broiler or gas grill or prepare a charcoal grill. Spray grill or pan with low-calorie cooking spray.

Using 4 skewers, carefully arrange the scallops on the skewers, alternating them with the peppers, mushrooms and onions.

Grill, turning once, for 5 minutes or until done. Serves 4.

Halibut with Celery & Peppers

1/2 cup natural almonds, coarsely chopped
4 halibut steaks, approximately 1 inch thick
freshly ground black pepper
flour for dredging
1 tablespoon low-fat margarine
2 tablespoons vegetable oil
2 peeled celery stalks, cut into 1 1/2 x 1/4 inch strips
1 sweet red pepper, cut into 1 1/2 x 1/4 inch strips

Preheat the oven to 350 degrees F. Place the chopped nuts on a baking sheet and toast in the oven for 5 minutes, stir once to turn.

Remove from the oven and set aside.

Season the halibut steaks on both sides with pepper. Dredge the steaks in the flour and shake off any excess.

Melt the margarine and vegetable oil together in a large skillet over moderately high heat. Add the halibut and cook until lightly browned, about 4 minutes per side. Arrange the steaks on a serving platter large enough to hold them all in a single layer. Keep warm.

Add the celery and red pepper to the skillet. Cook, stirring constantly, until tender, about 5-6 minutes, only add more oil if necessary.

Spoon the celery and red pepper over the halibut. Sprinkle with the toasted almonds. Serves 4.

Codfish with Crunchy Herb Coating

2 pounds codfish fillets
1/4 cup finely chopped pecans
1 cup bread crumbs
1 tablespoon chopped tarragon
freshly ground black pepper
2 tablespoons low fat milk
1 tablespoon Dijon style mustard

Preheat the oven to 400 degrees F. Line a baking sheet with aluminum foil and grease it with low-calorie cooking spray.

Place the pecans on a separate baking dish and toast in the oven for 3-5 minutes or until golden. Remove and allow to cool. Combine the pecans and bread crumbs, tarragon and black pepper.

Combine the milk and mustard in a small bowl. Brush the fish on both sides with the mixture. Dip each codfish fillet evenly into the bread crumb mixture, place on the baking sheet.

Bake in the oven for 15 minutes or until fish flakes easily and is golden. Serves 4.

Codfish with
Crunchy Herb Coating

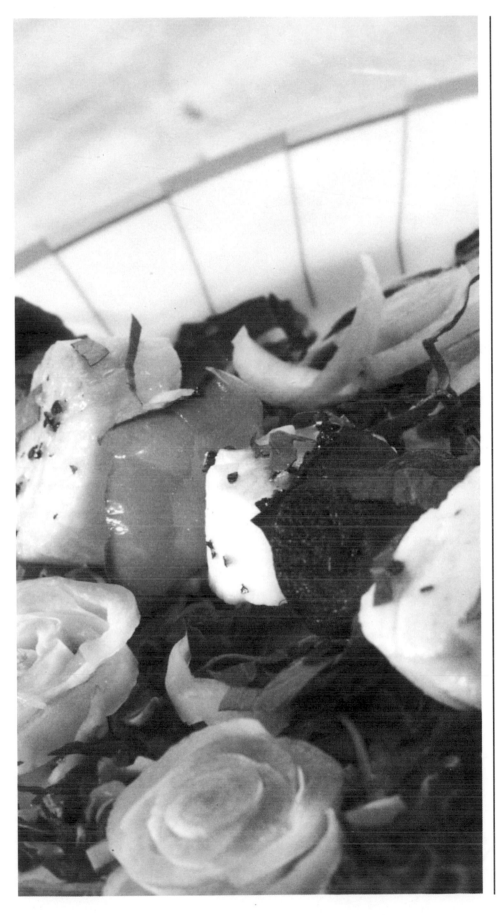

Grilled Skewered
Sea Scallops

90 | Chilled Mussels in Spicy Sauce

5 pounds mussels, scrubbed, cleaned and debearded
3/4 cup dry white wine
4 tablespoon olive oil
2 onions, very finely chopped
4 cloves garlic, minced
2 teaspoons ground cumin
2 pounds ripe tomatoes, peeled, seeded
    and finely chopped
2 35-ounce cans Italian plum tomatoes, drained
    and finely chopped
4 4-inch hot green chili peppers, seeded
    and finely chopped (wear rubber gloves)
1/4 cup finely chopped scallions
1/4 cup finely chopped fresh coriander

Put the wine into a heavy pot and add the mussels. Cover the pot and steam over high heat until the mussels open, about 5-8 minutes. Discard any mussels that do not open.

Using a slotted spoon, transfer the mussels to a large, shallow baking dish. Reserve the liquid. Remove the top shells from the mussels and discard them. Loosen the mussels from the lower shells, but leave them in the shells. Loosely cover the dish with damp paper towels and plastic wrap. Refrigerate for 4 hours or overnight.

Strain the reserved liquid into a bowl through a sieve lined with a double thickness of cheesecloth. Set aside.

Heat the olive oil in a skillet. When hot, add the onions and cook over a moderate heat until softened, about 5 minutes. Add the garlic and cook, stirring constantly until softened, about 2-3 minutes longer. Sprinkle the cumin over the onion and garlic, cook 1 minute longer, stir twice. Add the fresh tomatoes, canned tomatoes and 3/4 cup of the reserved cooking liquid. Bring the mixture to a boil. Reduce the heat and simmer, stirring constantly, until the sauce has thickened slightly, about 10 minutes.

Add the chili peppers and scallions, stir well. Remove from the heat and let the sauce cool. Add the chopped coriander and stir well.

Remove the mussels from the refrigerator and arrange on four individual serving plates. Spoon the sauce into individual bowls and serve with the mussels for dipping. Serves 4.

Warm Scallop Salad

2 ripe tomatoes
2 tablespoons olive oil
2 shallots, finely chopped
2 tablespoons fresh lime juice
1/2 teaspoon salt
1 teaspoon freshly ground pepper
2 tablespoons finely chopped fresh basil
1 pound sea scallops
freshly ground pepper, to taste
salt, if desired, to taste
2 bunches arugula, washed and stemmed

Halve and seed the tomatoes. Chop finely and set aside.

Heat the olive oil in a skillet over a medium heat. Add the shallots and sauté until soft, about 2-3 minutes. Stir in the lime juice, salt and pepper. Remove the skillet from the heat and add the tomatoes and basil. Stir well and set dressing aside.

Rinse and gently dry the scallops. Cut very large scallops in half.

Heat a large non-stick skillet. Add the scallops and sauté, turning frequently, for 3-5 minutes. Remove from the skillet and put the scallops into a large mixing bowl.

Add half the dressing to the warm scallops and season with additional salt and pepper. Toss well.

Distribute the arugula evenly among 4 plates. Top each plate with a portion of the warm scallops. Drizzle additional dressing over each portion. Serves 4.

92 | Grilled Tuna & White Bean Salad

1 1/2 pounds fresh tuna
1/2 cup fresh lime juice
2 teaspoons chopped garlic in oil
1 tablespoon fresh thyme
coarsely ground black pepper
1 large red onion, sliced thin
1 large can small white beans, rinsed and drained

DRESSING

4 tablespoons olive or vegetable oil
2 tablespoons tarragon vinegar
1 teaspoon Dijon-style mustard
1 clove garlic, minced
freshly ground black pepper

In a shallow dish combine the lime juice, garlic and thyme; stir to mix. Add the tuna turning several times to coat; sprinkle with coarsely ground black pepper. Allow the fish to marinate for at least 3 hours.

Preheat the broiler or gas grill or prepare a charcoal grill. Spray grill surface with low-fat cooking spray. Grill the tuna, 3 inches from heat source, for 3-5 minutes per side or until done. Remove from the grill and allow to cool to lukewarm.

Cut the tuna into large chunks and place in a serving bowl. Add the sliced red onion and drained white beans.

In a small jar or bowl combine the oil, vinegar, mustard, garlic and pepper, shake or mix well. Pour over tuna mixture and toss. Serve over or with greens if desired. Serves 4.